NEW COLOR SCHEMES MADE EASY

Better Homes and Gardens®

Meredith® Books

Des Moines, Iowa

NEW COLOR SCHEMES MADE EASY

Contributing Project Manager/Writer: Rebecca Jerdee
Contributing Editors/Stylists: Susan Andrews, Jeanne Blackburn,
    Bonnie Broten, Diane Carroll, Stacey Kunstel, Barbara Mundall, Robin Tucker
Contributing Graphic Designer: On-Purpos, Inc.
Copy Chief: Terri Fredrickson
Copy Editor: Kevin Cox
Publishing Operations Manager: Karen Schirm
Senior Editor, Asset & Information Management: Phillip Morgan
Edit and Design Production Coordinator: Mary Lee Gavin
Art and Editorial Sourcing Coordinator: Jackie Swartz
Editorial Assistant: Kaye Chabot
Book Production Managers: Pam Kvitne, Marjorie J. Schenkelberg, Mark Weaver
Imaging Center Operator: Kristin Reese
Contributing Copy Editor: Vicki Forlini
Contributing Proofreaders: Julie Collins, Sue Fetters, Michele Pettinger
Cover Photographer: Jay Wilde
Contributing Photographers: Laurie Black, John Reed Forsman, Joshua Savage
    Gibson, Bob Greenspan, Scott Little, Mark Lohman, Nancy Nolan, Jay Wilde
Contributing Indexer: Stephanie Reymann

Meredith® Books
Editor in Chief: Gregory H. Kayko
Executive Director, Design: Matt Strelecki
Managing Editor: Amy Tincher-Durik
Executive Editor: Benjamin W. Allen
Senior Editor/Group Manager: Vicki Leigh Ingham
Senior Associate Design Director: Doug Samuelson
Marketing Product Manager: Brent Wiersma

Executive Director, Marketing and New Business: Kevin Kacere
Director, Marketing and Publicity: Amy Nichols
Executive Director, Sales: Ken Zagor
Director, Operations: George A. Susral
Director, Production: Douglas M. Johnston
Business Director: Jim Leonard

Senior Vice President: Karla Jeffries
Vice President and General Manager: Douglas J. Guendel

Better Homes and Gardens® Magazine
Editor in Chief: Gayle Goodson Butler
Deputy Editor, Home Design: Oma Blaise Ford

Meredith Publishing Group
President: Jack Griffin
Executive Vice President: Doug Olson

Meredith Corporation
Chairman of the Board: William T. Kerr
President and Chief Executive Officer: Stephen M. Lacy
In Memoriam: E.T. Meredith III (1933–2003)

INTRODUCTION

With this book of beautifully schemed rooms as your springboard, you'll dive joyfully into the world of color. Here's what you'll discover:

The first chapter offers an overview of colors and their emotional effects on the psyche—you'll learn how much you already know as you take the quiz! Easy-to-understand color wheels and terms tell you how various hues work together. At the end of the chapter, you'll find five common starting points for developing color schemes.

Each succeeding chapter deals with one color and several of its variations. Large photos show how each combination works. The color key or palette accompanying each room shows the colors used and their relative proportions. If you want to duplicate the scheme, you'll know how much of each hue to use.

The final chapter, "Color for the Whole House," starting on page 168, takes creating color schemes to the next level. You'll see how to use a single palette to create color unity from room to room. Five houses exemplify five different ways to build relationships between the rooms of your home. Finally, turn to page 190 for the answers to nine frequently asked questions about choosing and using color.

Take a color leap! You'll be glad you did. This book makes it easy!

TABLE OF
CONTENTS

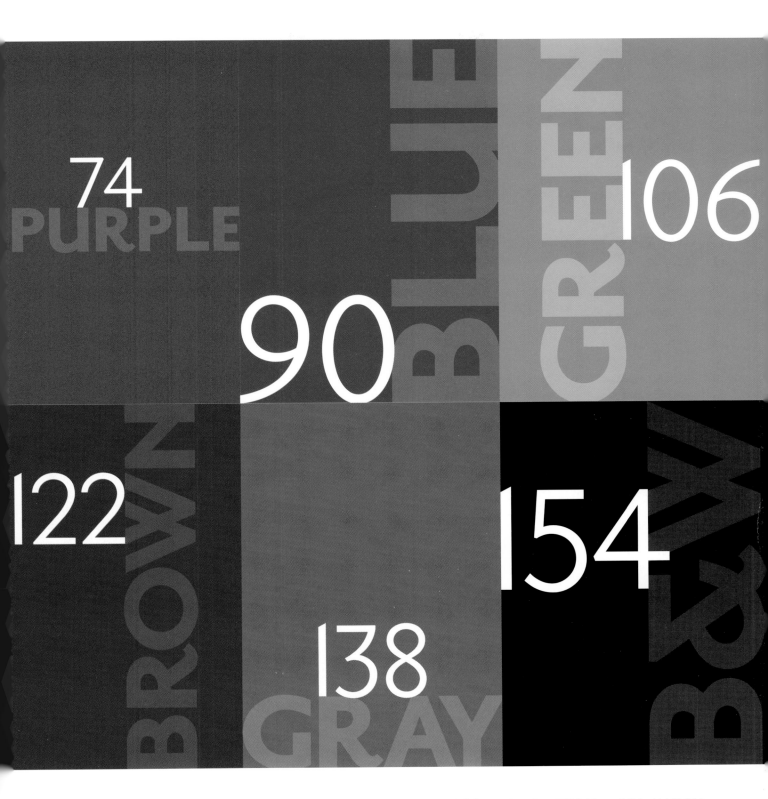

FOR THE LOVE OF COLOR

THE HEART RESPONDS TO COLOR

Whether you're drawn to a painterly palette of flamboyant hues or a paint box of watery pastels, your relationship with color has all the earmarks of an affair of the heart. It's primarily instinctive, emotional, and spontaneous. Simply put, color makes your world go around.

While you may not know why one color makes your heart beat faster than another or why a hue makes you run the other way, you can learn how colors work. This knowledge can boost your color confidence and help you choose schemes for your home that reflect and affect you and your family and how comfortably you live.

COLOR QUIZ:

10 THINGS YOU PROBABLY KNOW

No doubt you've heard the phrases "tickled pink," "green with envy," or "seeing red." Clichés common to Western culture, they reflect the sentiments attached to certain colors. Although a few hues have been shown to affect the heart rate, most color associations are culturally conditioned.

So how does your emotional knowledge of color compare with the general consensus? To find out, take the quiz below, filling in each blank with one of these answers: Red, Blue, Yellow, Orange, Green, Purple, Black, White, Brown, or Gray. You may discover that you know more about color than you thought you did!

1 _____, the color of quiet reserve, retreat, inactivity, and cool distance, takes a room away from the busy hubbub of a wild and colorful world. Associated with precious metals and weathered seashores, it's a classy and sophisticated way to neutralize a room. It associates well with any other color, so its uses are countless.

2 _____, the color of intellect and thought, promotes sunny feelings and a sense of well-being. Strong versions are said to stimulate the brain, aid clear thinking, and promote communication. Softer forms of the color are as warm and embracing as sunshine. The shades of this color make good choices for north-facing rooms.

3 _____, the up-for-anything color of dream and spirit, brings a sense of inner calm and inspiration to a room. In pale versions it makes a room appear larger, promoting contemplation or lighthearted fun. In pure, saturated forms it's royal, slightly off-the-wall, yet sophisticated.

4 _____, the color of health and vigorous growth, evokes feelings of renewal and hope. Research shows that when people look at this color, heart rates slow and people visibly relax. A walk in the woods helps connect with its restorative, healing qualities.

5 _____, the color of strength, night, and magic can strike fear into color schemers. Interior designers know its power to create drama, formality, sophistication, and contrast. For maximum emphasis use it to draw attention to furnishings, tie everything together, and underscore your color confidence.

6 _____, the pick-me-up color of heart, passion, and action, fills a room with emotional energy. Color therapists say it stimulates appetite and conversation, so it's often used in food advertising. In bold and gregarious tones, it seems to draw the walls of a room close, creating a cozy mood. Pastel versions set a more relaxing, nurturing, romantic tone.

7 _____, the mellow color of natural wood and earth, successfully bridges decorating gaps wherever needed. Associated with safety, security, and comfort, its warm neutrality surrounds a room like a hug that's not too passionate. Pale versions are expansive and reasonable; darker ones are dramatic and graphic. This color's laid-back tones work well at home in broken patterns and natural textures, just as they appear in nature.

8 _____, the color of calm, is the most popular color in American homes. It aids relaxation, honest communication, and sleep. Connected to sea and sky, it's associated with clear thinking and meditative environments. It's like a breath of fresh air, serene and restful. In dark versions it symbolizes strength, loyalty, and dependability.

9 _____, the color of cleanliness, innocence, and purity, can look clinical if not balanced with textures or other colors. Yet it refreshes, clarifies, and unclutters a room. It's associated with calm silence, like a landscape expanded after snowfall.

10 _____, the color of enthusiasm and sociability, elevates sensuality and strong feelings. It stimulates creativity, wraps a room with warmth and energy, and inspires optimism and self-confidence. The "it" color for the mid-2000s, it overcame its unflattering image from the late 1960s and 1970s.

Answers: 1. Gray 2. Yellow 3. Purple 4. Green 5. Black 6. Red 7. Brown 8. Blue 9. White 10. Orange

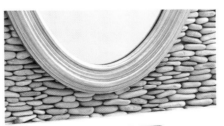

COLOR TALK:
CAN YOU FEEL THE HEAT?

WARM COLORS heat things up. They move forward in a room, communicate vigor, spread cheer, energize, stimulate appetites, promote excitement, and beg for attention. Yellow, orange, and red are the usual suspects, but sometimes purple, green, and blue come in warm, flirty tones if mixed with yellow or red.

The language of color uses hot, cold, warm, cool, or neutral words to describe how your body senses or visually "feels" temperature in a room. While these color words don't describe actual degrees of physical heat, they do try to explain color's effect on your physical well-being, activity level, and mood.

Some like it hot—rooms filled with bold, intense colors. Others prefer icy, reserved spaces of white, black, and gray. Most people like their rooms somewhere in between—warm, cool, or neutral. Check out the visual temperatures of these rooms.

Which temperature attracts you the most?

COOL COLORS, as the word implies, seem to lower a room's temperature. They step away, receding into the background. They're known for their passive natures and are useful for cooling you down, calming nerves, lifting spirits, and promoting contemplation. Most people find them soothing. Blue, green, and purple are usually labeled as cool, but red, yellow, and orange can also come in laid-back, calming tones if mixed with blue.

NEUTRAL COLORS (brown, gray, white, and black) create a room temperature somewhere in between warm and cool, depending on which hue you choose. Browns, such as taupe, cappuccino, khaki, or beige, symbolize a down-to-earth attitude and make you feel safe and secure. Grays, such as ash, granite, silver fox, or dove, work with all other colors to create spaces that are easy on the eyes. White can be as warm as cream or cold as snow, depending on whether it's mixed with red, blue, or yellow. And black? Black is basic, strong, the opposite of white. Mixed with white it becomes gray—a less powerful force in a room.

COLOR TALK:

ONE ROOM — THREE MOODS

CHEERFUL

The language of color is moody. Besides warmth, coolness, or neutrality, every color scheme can be described in terms of the ambience it creates in a room. Some schemes evoke the words "sophisticated," "formal," "earthy," or "dreamy." "Fresh," "complex," "simple," or "contemplative" are just a few more. The moods you can create are myriad, and each one can be interpreted in warm, cool, or neutral ways. When you choose a scheme, it's important to know what mood makes you comfortable or how you want to feel when you're in the room.

Here's what happens to a room in which upholstery never changes but the wall and accessory colors are altered to create three different moods:

CHEERFUL In the cheerful version (opposite) the room welcomes with a bright and sunny face. Its warm, simple color scheme uses color wheel neighbors—red and yellow—with a few neutral browns tossed in to allow breathing space.

CONFIDENT Warm but neutralized, the red and beige room (above right) feels more sophisticated than the yellow-walled room. Although the reds keep the room inviting and cozy, the mood has changed to something less vibrant or controversial (some people would find the cheerful space too warm). The color scheme uses related colors, but the neutrals take over more of the space, giving it a calmer feel.

SERENE Like refreshing mint, the green wall in the serene room (right) brings the ambience of the space into a cooler realm. The complementary red and green color scheme, made from color wheel opposites, sets up a sophisticated color play. The choice of a white-green instead of a yellow-green or dark green results in a semicool, relaxed atmosphere. The walls step back to allow the vibrant red of the sofa and chair to come forward as focal point colors in the room. Neutral zones (rug, ottoman, lampshade, and picture) settle in to accentuate the purer colors.

CONFIDENT

SERENE

COLOR TALK:
WORDS TO LIVE BY

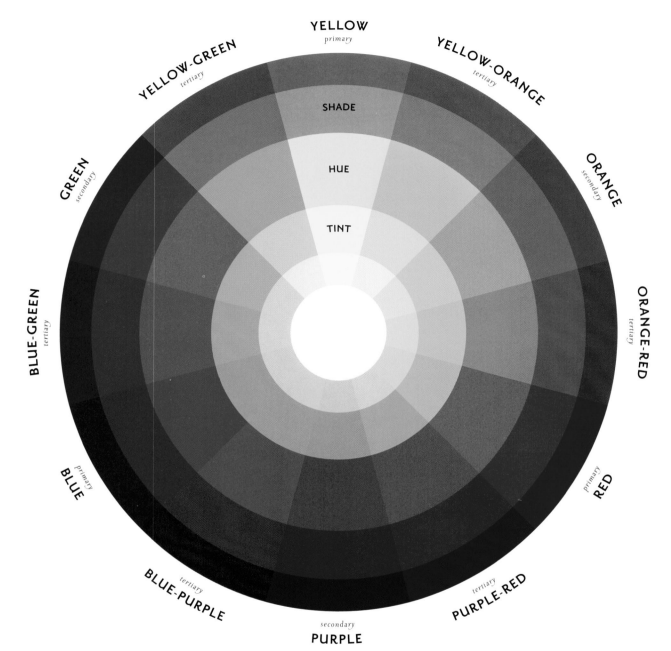

YELLOW
primary

YELLOW-GREEN
tertiary

YELLOW-ORANGE
tertiary

GREEN
secondary

ORANGE
secondary

BLUE-GREEN
tertiary

ORANGE-RED
tertiary

SHADE

HUE

TINT

BLUE
primary

RED
primary

BLUE-PURPLE
tertiary

PURPLE-RED
tertiary

PURPLE
secondary

The language of color includes the color wheel words illustrated by these drawings. The wheel—which may seem mysterious—is actually a simple and useful way to show how each color relates to the others. It's an invaluable tool to help you choose pleasing color combinations. Think of these words as Vocabulary 101, a basic knowledge of color that will stand you in good stead when creating color schemes or choosing one of the schemes you find in this book.

COLOR WORDS

The words **COLOR** and **HUE** are interchangeable. **PURE** hues are also known as **SATURATED,** meaning that they are intense, undiluted color. The word **INTENSITY** refers to a color's strength, while the **VALUE** is its lightness or darkness. Mixing pure hues with white creates light values called **TINTS,** while mixing them with black or other dark colors results in values called **SHADES.** The word **TONE** refers to either a tint or shade of a color.

PRIMARY colors—red, blue, and yellow—are the three basic colors from which all other colors are created. If you mix two primary colors, the result is a **SECONDARY** color: For example, red + blue = purple; blue + yellow = green; and yellow + red = orange. Purple, green, and orange are secondary colors. Going further, mixing a primary color and a secondary color next to it on the color wheel makes a **TERTIARY** color. Mixing a hue with its complement (opposite on the color wheel) softens and mutes the color, neutralizing it to a brown or gray.

COLOR SCHEME WORDS

MONOCHROMATIC refers to a scheme made up of one color and its various tints and shades. For example, a monochromatic scheme can come together with reds: pale or hot pinks, reds, and burgundy shades. A scheme created from colors next to each other on the wheel is called **ANALOGOUS** (above right). Because they share a common component, these colors always look good together. Opposites or **COMPLEMENTS** on the color wheel—red and green, orange and blue, or purple and yellow—form a **COMPLEMENTARY** scheme (center right). Opposite colors make each other look more intense. A **SPLIT COMPLEMENTARY** color scheme is made up of one color plus the two colors that are analogous to the first color's complement (below right). For instance, one split complementary is the combination of green + red-purple + red-orange. This may be too intense in pure forms but attractive in lighter or darker shades.

When any three colors are equally spaced on the wheel, they are called **TRIADS;** a color scheme composed of triads is balanced but somewhat overwhelming, so one of the colors should take precedence while the other two serve as accents.

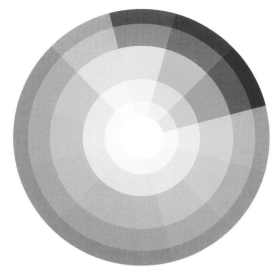

ANALOGOUS

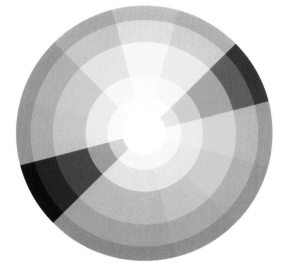

COMPLEMENTARY

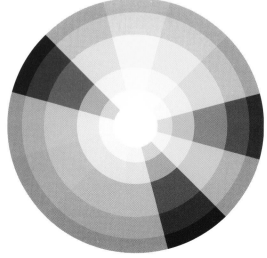

SPLIT COMPLEMENTARY

STARTING POINT: ART

The basics are in place: comfy furnishings, good floors, plenty of natural light. But the room still seems lackluster. The solution? An appealing art piece that gives the room a brand-new reason for being, expresses your personal taste, and provides a color palette to inspire new accessories. Draw the room's palette directly from a painting or print that is close to your heart. Choosing a wall color that's darker or lighter in tone than a dominant hue in the art emphasizes the piece as the room's focal point. This dining area in a combination living and dining space echoes the art on the wall with clever accessorizing in vivid orange, red, and cobalt blue. Notice how the intense hues of the accessories seem to float over the relaxed ocean blue wall, giving the room a balanced feeling.

CANVAS INSPIRATIONS *The contrast of the pastel wall behind the saturated intensities in the graphic paintings sets them off and makes them the attention-getters in the room. All other furnishings play secondary roles. The wall shelf becomes a display area for blue bottles and glassware with cobalt swirls that repeat the lines of the artwork.*

STARTING POINT: A FAVORITE COLOR

Does a particular color always make you feel good? If you have a favorite, it may be just the springboard you need for an entire color scheme. One way to make a palette is to use your favorite hue as the main element and add white, off-white, and one or two harmonizing colors as secondary elements and accents. For a monochromatic room, focus on one shade of the color and add darker and lighter versions of it in smaller amounts. Or use your favorite hue as a single color with neutrals.

This kitchen represents the third way to use a favorite color. The main color of the room, the sassy lime green of the cabinets, makes the whole kitchen sing. Whimsical and fun, the zesty hue sets a festive mood for cooking and entertaining. Granite countertops, wood flooring, white walls, and stainless-steel appliances are grounding neutrals.

HAPPY HUE *With an arresting saturated color like this brilliant yellow-green, you don't need a lot of detail and complexity to make the room interesting. Color alone creates focus.*

STARTING POINT: A CLASSIC COMBINATION

Color trends come and go, but certain color combos live forever. Always useful and comfortable, classic color pairings such as blue and yellow, blue and white, or red and white are reliable sources for color inspiration and an opportunity to experiment with proven color principles.

In this bedroom a blue and yellow duo teams with white for a Swedish take on cottage style. Framed by white, the two main colors of the bedding guide the choices for the wallcovering, wall and furniture paints, and window fabrics. Yellow, the background color of the focal point fabric, takes a background role on the wall. Blue, the color that defines the pattern in the fabric, underscores the lines of the room on the crown molding, wainscoting, window frames, and window muntins.

SWEDISH CHARM *This sunny look has elements that are hallmarks of Nordic style: natural light, painted surfaces, clean and simple fabrics. Bright and light, blue-and-yellow patterned bedding sets the room's scheme. Stripes and plaids are tried-and-true patterns for mixing with a focal point fabric.*

STARTING POINT: FABRIC

Draw color from a fabric you love. It's one of the easiest ways to pull together a color scheme. You really can't go wrong—after all, textiles carry ready-made palettes designed by professionals with knowledge of color.

You can use more than one pattern in a room, but for cohesiveness, each pattern should have one or more colors in common with the primary fabric. If some of the smaller accents are minor variations on the basic color scheme, that's OK—they keep the room from appearing contrived. The drapery fabric (left) inspired blue upholstery for the sofa, a green miniprint for an armchair, and a red plaid for a second chair. An orange rug gathers the seating pieces in a convivial arrangement, and the walls recede into the background with two pale hues borrowed from the fabric.

PATTERN INSPIRATIONS *The starting point for this room came from the curtain fabric, an exuberant print that unifies the space with a mix of all the room's hues. No single color is a standout on the print so fairly equal proportions are used in the room.*

STARTING POINT: A COLLECTIBLE

Who doesn't love to collect? Shoes, clocks, fabrics, books, and dishes top the list of collectors' favorite things. One or two of the same item isn't a collection, but when you add a third it is. If you have a collection, you hold the inspiration for a color scheme in your hands.

Brown and white transferware gave birth to the color scheme in this bedroom. The delicate patterns of the antique plates also suggested the same kind of traditional tracery on the fabrics. In this mostly monochromatic plan, light and dark variations of brown are collected and placed strategically throughout the room. White bedding and trimwork plus barely gray walls provide a neutral showcase for the combination of browns, fabrics, and transferware.

MIXED NOT MATCHED *Three different shades of brown in the transferware plates give the cue for a medley of browns in the bedding and furniture. The faded reds and greens of the floral chintz pick up the undertones of red and green in the various browns.*

YELLOW

Happiness and good cheer circle the room when you invite
yellow inside. Bright citrus and pistachio yellows wake you
up while the softer tones of vanilla, cream, and honey warm
you like sunshine. Yellow-greens add brightness, golds
glow with richness. Whatever your pick—buttercup, mustard,
bamboo, or lemon sherbet—yellow is sure to improve your
outlook on life.

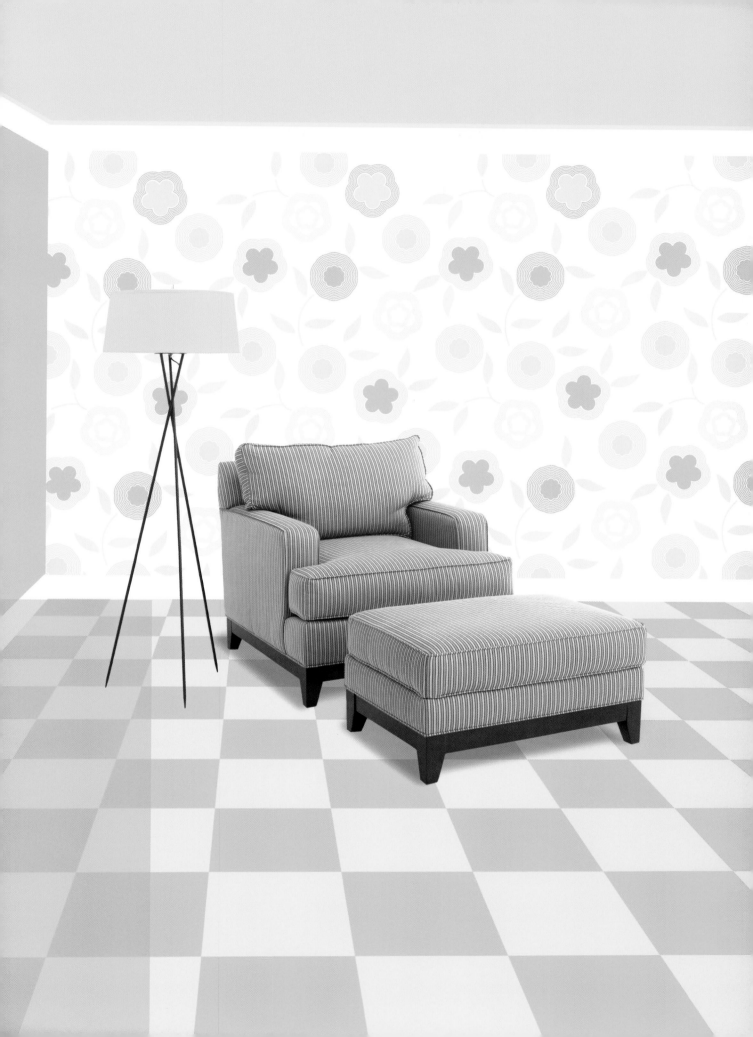

Well, hello, yellow!

You're bound to wake up with a sunny disposition in a bedroom filled with the color of sunshine. Yellow—in its simple, primary form—has natural associations with brightness, lightness, and a welcoming exuberance.

You can wrap an entire room in banana yellow, but if all the elements carry a similar level of intensity or value you'll be left with the impression that the room is fairly colorless. Well-placed shots of vivid coral wake up this yellow room and make it seem more vibrant.

Light patterning adds variety with toile and checks on bedding, buttoned backs on upholstery, and marbled designs on the fireplace and moldings. Small amounts of cream lift and lighten the intensity of the saturated hues.

COLOR KEY A. walls and draperies B. ceiling, trimwork, lampshades, bedding C. love seat and bedding D. mantel, carpet, and chair

o for the gold to gain richness and elegance for your rooms. An earthy variant of yellow, gold has chameleon qualities that sometimes let it appear yellow, at other times brown—it all depends on the colors you place next to it. For an easy-to-live-with color scheme, blend gold with neutrals. When framed by chocolate brown, caramel, cream, and snow white, gold glows like a warm sun. This huge living room feels cozy and unified with a striped tone-on-tone ocher-hue rug and a gathering of gold velvet upholstery pieces. Walls of windows dressed with brown silk draperies and white sheers set up a dramatic backdrop for staging the seating pieces.

Little pattern is used in this scheme aside from bold stripes on the rug and pillow and a paisley print on a chair and ottoman. With all the solid-color surfaces in the room, the patterned upholstery pieces become key accents that carry the colors of the scheme.

COLOR KEY A. rug, sofa, and love seat **B.** walls and sheer draperies **C.** draperies, chair, and pillows **D.** rug and chair **E.** pillow and chair

S oft yellows, combined with grays, tans, and taupe, create sophistication and simplicity no matter the furniture style of the room. In spaces graced with subtlety, shape and texture become more important to a decorating scheme. One shot of yellow on an accent wall in the living room (above) showcases the neutral furnishings. Lots of white—sofa, draperies, fireplace, lampshade, and platter—keeps the space airy while gray fabrics and blond woods add shape and texture.

Neutral-color furnishings are a good investment if you're fond of changing color schemes often. Paint is less expensive than new furniture, so you can celebrate every phase of life with a fresh coat of paint on the walls. In mostly neutral rooms a strategically placed jolt of yellow leaves the impression that more color is present in the room than actually is used.

COLOR KEY A. accent wall B. fireplace, sofa, draperies, lampshade C. chair upholstery D. pillows

To weave a warm cocoon for sleep, gather down-to-earth yellows. Sand-color paint combined with mellow-yellow oak and wheat-color sisals, silks, and velvets exudes security and abundance in this bedroom (below).

When pale colors collaborate they transform a room into a peaceful refuge. Limiting yourself to honeyed hues in varying tints and shades lets you focus on pulling together several contrasting textures, such as rough woods, smooth silks, and soft velvets, that will keep the room from appearing too dull. Smoky blue details, such as the long tapestry bed pillow and small ceramic flower vase, provide small touches of contrast in this cozy, barely yellow scheme.

COLOR KEY A. walls and bedding B. draperies, mirror frame, and rug C. tapestry pillows D. tapestry pillows, vase

COLOR KEY (opposite) A. walls B. cabinetry C. ceiling, moldings D. cupboards

COLOR KEY (above right) A. walls B. stain on chairs and cabinetry C. trimwork D. painting, wall in next room

Warm yellow, cool yellow. Which do you prefer? Compare the two color palettes (left). Both contain a yellow, a white, a red-brown, and a green. But notice how variations on these basic hues can produce quite different results. One kitchen feels warm and inviting because of rich, earthy colors that seem to step forward (opposite). The other gains cool sophistication from strong contrasts between a dark furniture stain and pale, barely yellow walls (above).

Choose your yellows carefully. If you're an uptown or urban type, you may prefer cool, reserved yellows mixed with a lot of white or a tint of gray. If you're a country-style person, check out spicy, saturated versions of sunshine yellow.

Pale but strong, thanks to patterned fabrics, this sitting room color scheme began with the elegant draperies that grace the doorway to the garden. The curtain fabric provides a ready-made color scheme suggesting hues for upholstery, painted walls, pillows, and artwork.

The room's yellow walls are a warm alternative to pure white, blending beautifully with the parchment background color of the draperies and providing a soft backdrop for twin art pieces. Because the colors in the room are close in value (lightness or darkness), the smooth and easy blend creates softness rather than contrast. Touches of coral, pink, and pistachio in similar values keep the scheme from becoming too sweet.

Tints, however, can turn a room into a cream puff. To keep a pale room from boredom, energize it with pattern. It kicks up a scheme in the way that texture keeps one-color schemes (pages 32–33) from dozing off. Start with one print that has a fairly large-scale design. Then add a plaid, a stripe, and a miniprint, all with colors relating to the color palette of the primary print. This room's upholstery does exactly that—the drapery and artwork carry large-scale designs while the chairs imitate the same colors with stripes on one chair, a soft miniprint on the other, and a big plaid on the ottoman.

COLOR KEY A. walls B. drapery fabric, art C. drapery and upholstery fabrics, art D. upholstery fabric E. floor tiles F. upholstery fabrics, art

COLOR KEY A. walls, trimwork, lantern B. furniture, pillows, lantern C. pillows, cushions, lantern D. pillows, rug, and cushions E. pillow trim

Fabrics with a yellow background led to the selection of raspberry-painted wicker furniture and colored lanterns on this lighthearted porch. You can create a similar scheme by starting with a fun fabric that takes you to the sunshine zone.

To play up the happy print, use it on the larger sections of upholstery cushions and accent pillows. Pull other colors from the print for pillow trimmings, such as the lime green and blue used here. Reserve the strongest contrasting color for high-intensity painted furniture pieces. The result is a lively scheme with bright colors in a variety of lights and darks.

Compare this dining room's color scheme to the color palette on page 37. They're essentially the same—yellow, white, pink, and green—with one big difference: brightness and clarity. The palette on page 37 is created from pinks and yellows with beige undertones, while the pinks and yellows here have white undertones that produce simpler, fresher impressions.

You could also compare the use of white in these rooms to the room on page 36. The proportions of white are different. Lots of white results in a light attitude here, while smaller portions of white yield a mellower look on page 36. Which room do you prefer?

COLOR KEY A. walls and rug B. trimwork, table, and chairs C. cushions, tablecloth, and rug D. artwork, tablecloth, and rug

Give any room a tropical punch. This spin of the color wheel stops at lemon zest and its flashy neighbors on each side—lime zing and tempting tangelo. Like lemons, limes, and tangerines in a fruit basket, these citrus colors roll together easily. These two rooms employ similar palettes—yellow, red-orange, and green—but in different proportions and with different accent colors to balance the strong hues.

In the sitting room (below), yellow and white serve as background colors that keep the stronger yellow, orange, and green in check. Red-orange appears throughout the space as an accent color, while the solid green chaises provide focus.

In the living room (opposite), a black rug anchors the scheme. Along with sconces, tiles, and dark wood furniture, the rug's hue grounds the tropical colors and gives the room depth and formality. The roles of green and red-orange are reversed in this room—red-orange is more important, balancing the saturated yellow of the walls and ceiling, and green plays a secondary role as a cooling accent. White woodwork also has a cooling effect.

If you're bashful about adding big colors to your rooms, start small—an accent wall, dishes on a tabletop, or a vibrant chair.

COLOR KEY (opposite) A. walls, ceiling B. upholstery C. rug, mantel tiles, and sconces D. upholstery and pillows E. trimwork, pillows, and mantel

COLOR KEY (left) A. side walls, floor, table, and draperies B. ceiling, draperies, and floor C. chaises and vases D. ottoman and back walls of bookcases E. bookcase surrounds and floor

ANGE

Step into a room where orange lives and you're likely to feel optimistic, self-confident, and energetic. Bright oranges demand center stage while peachy tones are quiet and flattering. Brick, burnt orange, and ginger give rooms a grounded, earthy base, while saffron, orange blossom, and peach champagne show a softer, subtler side of this fiery hue. Handle orange with care—it's hot!

Wow! It's a full-out, gutsy room that makes Code Orange a cause for celebration. The high-sheen paint-and-glaze hue on the walls has yellow and brown undertones that make a dramatic statement after hours. By day the deep color might overwhelm the space, but a white ceiling and trim and a creamy rug combine with sunlight pouring through large windows to keep the mood light and bright.

The antique mahogany table and chairs with their orange undertones warmly reflect the wall colors and complete the feeling of a warm embrace for those who dine at the table. Draperies and upholstery fabrics combine several demure orange tones without creating noisy patterns that could detract from the overall unity.

An old 1940s color rule states that soft oranges are wonderfully warming while darker ones must be used in smaller proportions. This room is proof that modern colors and new applications let you go confidently beyond the old rules to enjoy the full-blown pleasures of a glorious and radiant color.

COLOR KEY A. walls B. draperies C. trimwork and ceiling
D. table and chairs E. rug

S tir a juicy color scheme with fruity oranges, tangerines, pears, and a twist of lime. You'll get a taste for this flavorful palette if you use white and black to give the high-energy colors space to shine. Trust natural light to illuminate the hues and hang big mirrors to bounce light around the room.

This born-beige condo surrendered its industrial look to exuberant oranges and yellows that climb its 10-foot-high walls. The life-giving colors invigorate the tall spaces and visually expand the narrow rooms. Staying true to the lightness and brightness of the plan, white furniture breaks up the saturated palette and sets off the colors. The large white living room sofa frames accent pillows that repeat the scheme in small, snappy color blocks. A neighbor on the color wheel, apple green adds an offbeat surprise to the analogous orange and yellow scheme.

COLOR KEY A. walls B. pillows C. sofa, trimwork, and accessories D. draperies and pillows E. end tables and frames F. vase and end tables G. rug

COLOR KEY A. walls and sofa B. pillows C. coffee table and rug D. chairs E. art F. end tables

Orange comes in many guises. If lightened with white, it's peachy. If you add a lot of yellow, it becomes marigold. The addition of blue creates gray and a bit of black added to orange produces the color of clay or red earth.

Unlike the bold oranges on the walls of the two previous rooms in this chapter, orange's part in this room is subtle and small. This color scheme takes its cues from the painting hung over the sofa. Rust and terra-cotta tones (earthy versions of orange made by mixing it with black) appear in small amounts in the painting, while warm neutrals cover the largest areas. Note how the dark lines of the painting are repeated on the rug and the tables, giving the room a linear quality. The walls, sofa, and chair upholstery echo the painting's neutral hues, taking a dominant role in the room, while the rusty orange pillows on the sofa draw the eye as an accent color.

Harmonious palettes made of colors adjacent to each other on the color wheel are always successful. This orange and barely yellow palette has an intrinsic bond. No matter what proportions you use with these hues, the space where you place them will generate comfort and ease.

COLOR KEY (left) A. bed quilt B. bed, table, and wallpaper C. wallpaper, linens, and accessories D. quilt E. lampshade, bedding, and flowerpot

Feeling adventurous? Dare to pair complementary colors. Blue, orange's complement, gets you started. Use a variety of blues—from sea foam to deep navy—with accents of orange. The bedroom (above) begins with major pieces in blue laced with generous amounts of white for a light and airy look. Orange accents stir up excitement in small amounts. For a livelier look reverse the plan. Make orange dominate and use blue to accent.

A handmade Caribbean-style headboard (opposite)—displaying a painter's palette of geometric shapes in ginger-peach, aqua, green, robin's egg blue, and white—inspired the use of similar colors for the rest of the room. A gingery-orange accent wall, red-orange African-motif fabrics, and a West Indies-inspired lamp combine in a tropical synthesis of cultures and color. A white cotton matelassé bedspread and white wicker furniture contrasts with the sizzling colors, making the room appear balanced, clean, and inviting.

COLOR KEY (opposite) A. wall B. pillows, rug, and headboard C. bedding, nightstand, headboard D. headboard E. headboard

50

Deep colors and sumptuous textures beckon from this inviting room. A soft mix of fabrics—silk, chenille, velvet, and taffeta—combines with a spicy blend of modern and global furnishings. A little more on the unexpected side, the scheme curves around a warm section of the color wheel. From orange and red-orange to red-violet and violet, the hues assemble an easy-to-use analogous scheme that's compatible with dark woods, woven wicker, and collectible baskets.

A ripe melon shade on one wall beckons guests who might gather in this convivial space and partners with lavender walls. The pairing of lavender and peach invites a darker purple for draperies. Anchored by a section of dark brown and gray carpet fastened into the laminate flooring, the gutsy cranberry sectional sofa wraps the room in comfort and intimacy.

When using this scheme, choose a variety of light and dark colors. The light colors keep the dark hues in check and ensure that the room doesn't become too heavy or oppressive. Remember the old principle that says dark colors move in on spaces, making them feel smaller and cozier? It's still true.

COLOR KEY A. seating B. wall, lamp, bookcase, trimwork C. wall D. rug E. tables and rug F. draperies

O range, known for its ability to energize conversation and sociability—as well as the appetite—dines here with grace. Kept to a minimum, a low-intensity orange pairs with soft gray walls and warm, sunny yellows to embrace the natural light pouring through grand windows. Elegant, softly patterned orange and yellow fabrics carry the palette by way of upholstery, draperies, and rugs.

In such a subdued color scheme, other elements are needed for detail and interest. For example, the antique French crystal chandelier, a centerpiece of the space, adds refinement, curves, and the room-elevating glitter of crystal. The shine of gold is another important element that is found on sconces, the chandelier, and picture frames.

Even place settings and flowers can align with a room's color scheme to maintain the overall harmony. Here the table settings—crystal stemware and elegant cream and gold china—echo the chandelier while a tabletop centerpiece of melon-color roses and eucalyptus branches adds natural freshness and a finishing touch to the dining room space.

COLOR KEY A. walls and chair frames B. draperies, pillows, and chair upholstery C. trimwork, sofa, and ceiling D. sofa E. pillows

Pink and orange, an exotic pairing so adored in the 1960s by peace-loving flower children, are back with global connotations perfect for outdoor living in the 21st century.

To keep up with the alfresco decorating trend, weather-worthy fabrics are available in a growing array of colors and patterns. Now you can mix hues such as pomegranate, wine, fuchsia, and tangerine with the global patterns of India, Morocco, or Jamaica. Pair textured pieces with floral or allover patterns like these to bring soft style to the hard edges of your garden, patio, or backyard. Outdoors you can count on the blue-greens of plants (the natural complement of these red-oranges) to cool down the steamy-hot scheme.

The easiest way to pair hot pinks with hot oranges is to keep them close in value—and not too light or too dark. A good practice is to compare paint strips with graduating values. You'll find good pink and orange combos at the same levels when lining up two strips. To choose fabrics, match fabric swatches using the squint test. With your eyes nearly closed, see if the fabric swatches are close in value. If one seems to "jump out," choose something darker or lighter until you find a closer value. Try the squint test on the pink and orange color swatches below to see how this works.

COLOR KEY A. cushions B. cushions C. table and accessories D. cushions and concrete flooring E. stones in concrete flooring

Whether you call it cranberry, raspberry, or crimson, red brings boldness, passion, and energy to rooms. You'll feel warmer in a red room because the intensity of the color affects your energy level and makes you feel vibrant and alive. Pinks—reds lightened by white—set a more relaxed, nurturing tone. Get to know your reds before committing to one. It's a special kind of love affair.

RED

Even a small detail can suggest a color scheme. This dining room's rich red wall color echoes the rooftop in the painting hung to the left of the arched doorway. A simple scheme of one bright color (red) plus neutrals (white, gold, and brown) dazzles the cozy space. Dining here feels warm, intimate, and comfortable.

When painting a wall red, you'll need many coats of paint unless you prime the wall properly. The secret to preparing for a vivid red: Buy a primer mixed with black pigment to hide the previous color.

Use a warm white paint on adjacent walls to make this garnet red tone sing and to give the eye places to rest from the intensity of the color. Note how the white paint breaks at the edge of the arched doorway, defining the architecture of the room and visually opening the entry space beyond.

When using a dramatic red, it's a good idea to keep draperies, fabrics, and design details (such as frame styles or hardware) simple to avoid visual overload. Gold frames become part of the "jewelry" of the room, and the chairs are slipcovered with economical and washable white cotton, keeping the strong red color from overwhelming the senses of those seated at the table.

COLOR KEY A. wall, artwork B. entryway walls, slipcovers, and accessories C. artwork D. artwork

Fire up an urban space with spicy versions of red and yellow. Finish off the room by cooling the spice with a sleek, uptown gray. Most lofts tend to project a cold and austere feeling, with high ceilings, exposed systems, concrete beams, and ductwork. The trick is to treat these elements in ways that make them friendly and fun. In this lofty home the space is undivided by walls; furniture placement defines the living and dining spaces. Turning the back of the sofa toward the dining table creates a visual barrier to stop the eye. For intimacy, a red wall sets a warm tone for the entire space, and the lower two-thirds of the adjacent wall is covered with wood paneling (the top of the paneling aligns with the horizontal lines of the windows). Mustard yellow tops the paneling, giving the eye a place to soar.

Furniture colors play off those on the walls: Red upholstered dining chairs draw out the warmth in the brown paneling; gray upholstery in the living room contrasts with the red wall; and two stacked chests behind the sofa summarize the color scheme.

COLOR KEY A. wall and chairs B. wall C. divider wall, buffet, appliances, and sofa D. wall paneling and cabinetry

COLOR KEY A. bedding, secretary, lamp, accessories
B. walls C. chair and draperies D. bedding and trimwork
E. raffia carpet

This bedroom successfully combines bright colors and bold patterns. It begins with plain, pale blue walls that create a restful backdrop for sleeping. White trim is part of the whole house scheme, and raffia carpet puts light color and casual texture underfoot.

Adjacent to the bedroom, the hallway's wallpaper suggests a flow of pattern and color into the room. Red and blue plus a few neutrals unlock the scheme—blue for the mostly cool space, red for warmth, and neutrals for pauses between strong colors. Tall sweeps of blue-and-white pattern define the windows, and a vivid peacock blue chair pairs with a red secretary. Red and white stripes, wonderful for sorting through paisleys and miniprints, define the bed backdrop.

Unsure about your tolerance for strong patterns and bright colors? Start small. Begin with a lampshade or bedding. Hold off on expensive items such as wallpaper until you know your limits.

Some like it hot, hot, hot. Fuchsia, red, and white—the wow combo—is a hit with some crowds. When you choose to make a bright, bold room such as this, you're a creative type, an emotional exhibitionist open to the world of color scheming and craving the joy and energy of strong hues.

For balance, apply the three main colors in fairly equal proportions. This room started with a wonderful pink and white-dotted rug that set a modern tone on a white-painted floor. Fuchsia walls echo the rug. Three horizontal bands of red—a sofa, sideboard, and hanging cupboard—anchor the room. To relieve and balance the intensities of the pinks and reds, bring in white (suggested here by the rug's dots) on tables, lamps, side chairs, trim, curtains, and wall lights. Choose silver as the color for metals.

To add more verve to the scheme, toss in orange accents on tabletops and fabrics.

COLOR KEY A. walls and rug B. sofa, storage, and accessories C. tables, chairs, floor, rug, curtains, trimwork, and lamps D. furniture, mirrors, and curtain rods

When you think life is too short to be beige, you're in good company. Color lovers see hues as an indispensable part of their lives. If you agree, a brilliant red will add warmth and richness to your spaces. This bedroom began with the designer pushing for some "good rich color" to alleviate the modern room's bare white walls and neutral furnishings. The cherry red on the walls actually preceded the artwork; the painting then led to color choices for the textured bedding and accent pillows.

Finding the right red may require a few trials, so plan to experiment with large test swatches painted on sample boards you can view under natural and artificial lighting. One clue for success may be the wood that's already in the room. The cherry wood here suggested a warm-tone red. Once the walls are coated, you can cool down red's visual heat with blue-green and crisp white accents.

COLOR KEY A. walls B. duvet cover and pillows
C. carpet D. bedding, trimwork, and light fixtures

COLOR KEY (right) A. walls, pedestal, pillows, sofa, lampshade, and rug B. sofa, pillows C. rug, curtains, sofa, and pedestal D. curtains E. rug, lamp base

COLOR KEY (opposite) A. wall and bedding B. bedding C. bedding and pillows D. bedding, curtain, and accessories E. trimwork, lamp, and tables

Tickled pink and green? If the bedroom scheme (opposite) gives you a thrill, you'll find lots of inspiration for wall colors in comforters, pillows, fabrics, and bedding items at retail stores. The success of the pink-dominant scheme comes from mixing patterns and adding white accents and a touch of green. Vary the scale and concentration of the patterns by mixing solids, allover designs, and geometric pieces to keep the room interesting.

Pink and chocolate—a color trend with staying power—is exciting because pink takes brown from boring to delicious. In its myriad shades (soft petal to punchy coral), pink sweetens and invigorates brown. The room (above) balances pink and brown, pairing them in a variety of patterned fabrics. If you don't want pink to rule, use it sparingly as an accent color—in a rug, on a wall, on a lampshade, or in a multicolor fabric.

COLOR KEY A. masonry, tile, and rugs B. upholstery, tablecloth, door, drapery, and umbrella C. wrought-iron furniture D. accessories E. frames and pots F. fabrics

I f you're country French at heart, bring the Provençal palette outdoors for life under blue, blue skies. The organic hues of the French countryside take their cues from nature: sky blues, a bright yellow sun, reddish soil, and lush green vineyards. Let the sky be your ceiling, your plantings the vineyard greens. All you need to do is decorate with red and yellow!

This outdoor living space works around an existing exterior of earthy content—stone walls and brick red trim—that suits a country French decorating style. Black wrought-iron furniture sets the stage for Provençal hues.

To decorate, choose red-and-cream farmhouse checks, plaids, floral prints, and solids for upholstery fabrics, draperies, and tablecloths. Then pop in a bright yellow-and-red accent print on lampshades or other accessories. Repeat the reds and yellows on garden pots to underscore the color scheme and maintain unity.

Tints and shades of purple fill rooms with dream and spirit—some soft as a whisper, others as dramatic as a Pavarotti opera production. The serene tones of periwinkle, lilac, and lavender unlock the doors of calm, expansive spaces that let you float away on a cloud. If that's not what you're in the mood for, find passion and excitement in deeper purples like violet, iris, eggplant, and plum. What shade of purple are you?

PURPLE

Banish the notion that lavender belongs only to little girls or grandmothers. Lavender may be just the hue you need to cast a darkened room in a whole new light. The soft purple framing this upstairs suite lifts the room out of its doldrums, leaving it with a color that encourages rest and relaxation.

To cut the femininity associated with lavender, give it a masculine edge by pairing it with black. The impressive four-poster and tall dresser in this room add strength and solidity to the scheme. Notice how the dark-stained French doors are kept in check with white frames. Season the room with a bold accent color that's one step away from yellow, lavender's complement. Lime green fabric on the sofa mixes with solid, stripe, and plaid pillow patterns. Elegant bedding adds to the room's frill-free maturity.

COLOR KEY A. walls, bedding, and pillows B. walls, trimwork, and accessories C. dresser, doors, and bed frame D. sofa

COLOR KEY A. walls B. upholstery, draperies, and accessories C. upholstery D. pillows E. draperies, lampshades, and trimwork

I f you've never used the color purple, try it—you might like it. Gather paint chip samples from a paint store or home improvement center to decide which ones please you most. Match the shades—blue-purples to red-purples and light purples to dark purples—in a color play that will teach you what you like best. The range from pale pink-lavender to deep blue-plum is vast. You can create whole room schemes from the nuances of purple alone.

These rooms play both sides of the purple spectrum, resulting in two different moods. One is calm and restful, the other proposes conviviality. The walls of the sitting room (below) were first painted with a pale pinkish lilac and then color-washed with a mix of clear glaze and a darker version of the same hue. Blue-purple fabrics on draperies and cushions contrast with the reddish purples, while taupe and white add breathing space.

In a room for the bold and the beautiful, the walls of the dining area (above) are lined with purples—blue-purple sheers and red-purple curtain panels tied back to lavender walls. Like a bit of theater, the dramatic decorating is a stage for great conversation.

To add vitality to a primarily purple space, use pale and bold versions of yellow, purple's complement. Here a pale gold rug carries hints of purple that reflect the stronger purples of the other fabrics. An intensely vibrant yellow painting stands out as an accent piece.

What keeps this color scheme from drifting away? Dark brown. Like a secure anchor, the room is grounded by dark picture frames, curtain rods, and furniture pieces.

COLOR KEY A. walls and draperies B. draperies and upholstery C. carpet D. chairs and table E. artwork

A storm cloud of violet tempered with tobacco brown creates a bedroom setting where you can rest your head in opulence and drama. In a daring display of olive greens against a warm purple accent wall, this bedroom is the lap of luxury.

So what's the secret of the style? It's the confident mix of rich color and sumptuous textural fabrics: pale taupe silk draperies, a shiny taffeta duvet cover, luscious eggplant pillows, a deep velvet fringed throw, a leather bench, and a graphic area rug. A tobacco color on side walls warms the large spaces and visually lowers the ceilings. Crisp white trimwork contrasts with the deep colors, brightening the scheme. Yellow picture mats call attention to the purple focal-point wall. The entire look is clarified further with the outlining effect of black on the lamp base and rug border.

COLOR KEY A. walls and ceiling B. carpet and draperies C. upholstery, pillows, and throw D. accent wall E. picture mats F. bedding and rug G. rug and lamp base H. trim and lampshades

COLOR KEY (left) A. ceiling B. wall panels C. walls
D. draperies E. trimwork F. upholstery, rug

Purple and yellow complementary schemes can be as different as night and day depending on their intensity (color saturation) and value (color lightness or darkness). These rooms illustrate two extremes.

In the dining room (above) the lavender ceiling adds a plain, serene element to a complexly furnished space. Coupled with pale yellow walls, the ceiling also helps balance the weight of dark furnishings and links the room to sunny windows. The dramatic living room (opposite) pairs intense versions of purple and yellow to make a bold color statement and an intimate salon for conversation.

Here's a good rule: Complementary colors look best when they're fairly equal in intensity and value. Use pale with pale and deep with deep.

COLOR KEY (opposite) A. walls, ceiling B. draperies and pillow C. upholstery, curtain rods, picture frame, and rug D. tablecloth and accessories E. trimwork, lamp, chandelier, and accessories F. chandelier shades G. pillows H. upholstery

Cottage styles are sweet and easy to live with, especially when blessed with garden-fresh colors. What does "fresh" mean to a color palette? Look for clear, pure colors that aren't muted by black or neutralized by a complement. Pastels—pure hues diluted by white—fall within the garden-fresh realm too.

While you stand in front of the myriad choices at the home improvement center, it helps to know that paint companies develop three types of colors: pure saturated hues (yellow, orange, red, purple, blue, and green), diluted variations (colors made by mixing pure saturated hues with white to make pastels), and muted variations (complex colors made by mixing pure saturated hues with white, black, and/or their complements to get neutralized, less

COLOR KEY A. walls, floor, furniture, and tablecloth B. wall, floor, and tablecloth C. tablecloth and seat cushions D. seat cushions

COLOR KEY A. wall, fabrics B. trimwork, chairs, wall art, fabrics, rug C. rug, wall art, upholstery D. table

intense colors). When looking for a cottage-style palette like the one in the eating area (opposite), choose pure saturated hues, pure white, and those diluted with white.

This eating area (below) has a more complex palette—the colors are muted a bit by black or a complement. Compare the beige undertones of these colors to the white undertones of the simple hues in the room opposite. Also note the role of beige as the neutral in the room below versus the role of white in the other.

Lilac walls create quiet backdrops in both rooms, but the eating area gets a perk-up from a large dose of yellow-green (yellow is purple's natural complement). The multicolor fabrics suggested purple and green as the main colors for painted furniture. With coordinated plaids and stripes for patterns and visual interest, the main colors act as frames for the fabrics.

L oft or basement rooms are perfect places to experiment with rough-and-tumble color schemes. Open ceiling rafters and concrete floors and walls beg to be covered with something that will lift the space from its basic-box look to lively, livable quarters. Here's a room with a youthful, industrial style that begins with corrugated metal and plywood paneling on the walls. No attempt is made to hide the methods for the wall construction.

To color such a neutral space, dare to pair purple with lime green, a popular color trend. The intense versions of the duo shown here take the scheme to eye-popping levels. Played against the walls, the strong, saturated colors are positively riveting, vibrant, and energizing. Note how the bright color painted on the concrete floor makes a bold backdrop that offsets the dark upholstered furniture.

To turn this decorating duo into a split-complementary color scheme and give your room even more zing, add orange. Here a few flowers and pieces of fruit hint at what could happen. For more permanent effects, add an orange painting, pillows, or rug.

COLOR KEY A. upholstery, rug, and accessories B. floor, side table, throws, and accessories C. wall and accessories D. plywood wall, shelving, and curtains

Do you let your ceilings languish in white? Unleash their power with color. If you're in a deep purple mood, prepare for a dramatic change that will bring the ceiling—a fifth wall—much closer. When painting with deep colors, remember to prime first with a black-tinted primer to cut back on the number of paint coats necessary for a smooth finish.

The deep blue-violet that covers the walls of this small, square bedroom crosses the ceiling to create a unified, dramatic backdrop for fiery fabrics in intense lime greens, hot pinks, and oranges. To create a two-tone ceiling like this, first paint it with the wall color. Using painter's tape, mask off the ceiling in a harlequin pattern. Repaint the ceiling in a metallic purple paint a shade lighter than the base color. A snappy white chandelier with hot pink shades creates a bright, inspiring centerpiece.

A triad color scheme—three colors equally spaced on the color wheel—is balanced but somewhat overwhelming, so one of the colors should take precedence while the other two serve as accents. In this case blue-violet gets the lion's share of coverage while the yellow-greens and pink-oranges accent the space in small, vibrant bites. Use white to separate intense colors or to keep them from running together.

COLOR KEY A. walls and ceiling B. draperies, pillows, wall art, and accessories C. draperies, bedding, wall art, rug, lampshades, and accessories D. carpet E. bedding, chair, lampshades, and accessories F. door, shutters, and accessories

Like sea and sky, blue is ever-changing—one minute it's bright and airy, the next it's cloudy and gray. Yet you can always count on blue to create a calm, restful room. Choose cornflower or aquamarine blues for sweet or celestial spaces. For crisp or casual moods, bring china blue or sapphire into a room. Indigo blue adds an exotic flair, while navy blue connotes security and trust.

B

What moody blue are you? For surefire success with color scheming, pair your favorite tint or shade of blue with white. Whatever your choice, it's a classic combo that always works.

Say your favorite blue falls in the strong, dark range—a blue with power, a color you trust. For you, the sumptuous flourish of marine blue circling this banquet table is a feast for the eyes. The powerful, solid, and friendly scheme begins on the floor, where a sea of sculptured blue Tibetan carpet interrupts the contrast between white walls and dark hardwood floors. Floating upward, the color washes over chairs in striped denim slipcovers. This bold blue has staying power, thanks to the noncompetitive white walls that set it off. To keep the room from seeming stark, add meaningful blue-and-white accessories and subtle beige fabrics.

COLOR KEY A. rug and upholstery B. walls, chandelier, and tablecloth C. vases and wall art D. table underskirt and draperies

COLOR KEY (right) A. walls B. trimwork, bedding, and painted chest C. carpet, decorative pillows D. ceiling E. painted chest F. pillow and lampshade trims

COLOR KEY (opposite) A. walls B. ceiling, door, trimwork, wicker, bedding, pillows C. quilt, pillows

s it blue or is it gray? Gentle Gray was the color choice for the bedroom (above), but when applied to the walls, it looks positively blue. The lesson? You may find just the right blue in the gray section of the color chip rack at the paint store.

The cloudy gray-blue hue has a reserved, cool quality that's as urban as a white dress shirt, gray wool slacks, and stilettos. Taupe paint lowers the ceiling over the bed alcove for an intimate mood, while white trimwork delineates the complex, grayed-down hues. The room's air of sophistication is supported by the space-heightening four-poster bed dressed in crisp white bed linens. Soft blue chambray pillow shams and tapestry pillows add pops of color to the bed.

Casual as a white T-shirt and blue jeans, the country-style bedroom (opposite) gathers the sweet and innocent aspects of blue. Pale periwinkle walls framed by white trimwork and a white ceiling are careful not to intrude on the room's small space. White linens and furniture add to the ethereal quality of the room. The blue and white of the patchwork quilt and pillows made from dish towel fabric welcome you into a calm and restful retreat.

D o salty sea breezes call your name? Even without the ocean at your door, you can enjoy a seaside decorating style. This room started with blue wall paint the color of the ocean on a gray day. A darker blue was sponged over it for a smoky cast. A 16-inch-wide band of white stands in for more expensive crown molding, brilliantly setting off the aqua-blue ceiling. White trim frames the doors, windows, and walls for a crisp, well-defined look.

To keep the room from feeling ice-cold, the soft textures of the pillows and the whisper-soft folds of the floor-to-ceiling draperies contrast with the slick, painted surfaces. Lest the room drift away, anchoring elements appear near the floor: Drapery borders line up with the bottoms of the window frames, fading to gray at the carpet. Black punches up the scheme on a mirror and table, adding strength and weight.

COLOR KEY A. walls, sofa B. ceiling, pillows
C. trimwork, doors, lampshade, pillows D. ottomans, pillows,
large pot E. carpet, draperies, pillows, sofa cushion F. mirror
frame, table, ottomans

t takes two main colors to tango your way to a successful room scheme. If you use more than two, you'll be in a rainbow world or trying to balance a triad scheme. So for the sake of simplicity, just pick two. Then, to keep the scheme interesting and engaging, add neutrals as well as lighter, darker, warmer, or cooler versions of the two main colors.

Blue and yellow, a common, compatible, and cheerful pair, have delighted home decorators for centuries. In this dining room (opposite), blue and yellow unify a collection of 1950s pottery. The honey hue of the vintage furniture and mellow blond color of the floor can be considered cousins to the yellow of the chair upholstery. Turquoise walls provide a cool backdrop for the warm fabric and woodtones, and neutral whites mediate between the warm and cool hues.

The bedroom (above right) expresses the same blue and yellow theme but explores a stronger use of neutrals. Cool black and white graphic patterns contrast with the mellow yellows, soft creams, and wood elements, creating a more contemporary look than that of the retro-style dining room.

COLOR KEY (opposite and above) A. walls, dishware, blanket, and accessories B. seat cushions and bedding C. ceiling, curtains, and pillows D. pillows and bed curtains

You can't go wrong with basic furnishings in neutral colors. They'll collaborate with any color scheme and make the hues pop. These basics—tan sofa, wood coffee table, pendent lamp, metal lamp, laminate flooring, and woven wicker seating pieces—woke up one day to blue and orange accents.

What makes this room inviting is the range of midvalue colors that create a light and airy mood. From blue to green and yellow to orange, the colors fall in the same range of midtones. The only dark element, the coffee table, provides a necessary anchor. Most of the colors on the patterned surfaces are laced with white for additional coolness. The color scheme softly recedes, enlarging the sense of space. Doses of yellow-orange, pale blue's near-complement, add an uplifting, sunshiny note.

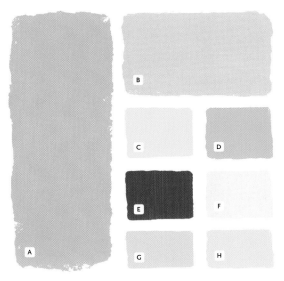

COLOR KEY A. walls and accessories B. upholstery, wicker, chandelier C. pillows D. pillows, side table, accessories E. rug, accessories F. trimwork, rug, accessories G. pillows, accessories H. pillows

Compare the blue-and-orange scheme (opposite) to the one on pages 100–101. In this room stronger oranges paired with blues and neutrals drum up a livelier mood. The red-orange duvet cover and pillows in the bedroom (right) have a similar effect. The orange complements in these rooms make focal points that gently push blue into the background.

Still, blue is in command. In the room (opposite) blue defines an office in a closet, opening up the living space and inviting you in. Blue, known for its calming qualities, sets a quiet mood for working, while the orange lampshade suggests a bright light for ideas.

You can count on light blues to breathe fresh air into a sleeping space (right). Their receding qualities seem to expand the volume of the room, letting you feel that the sleeping space is bigger than it really is. It cools the atmosphere, making room for dreams, while yellow draperies add a sunny effect.

COLOR KEY (opposite) A. wall, desk, rug B. wall, draperies, accessories C. draperies, table, lamp D. seat cushion, lamp E. runner, lampshade, accessories F. draperies

COLOR KEY (above) A. walls B. bedding, seat cushion, curtains, and accessories C. trimwork, ceiling, chest of drawers, and accessories D. curtains

Ah, room for a view! Picking colors for outdoor rooms depends on the architecture and the surrounding setting. Because white architecture goes with any color, the vista from the porch (above) guided the color scheme toward the blue-greens, blues, and greens of the natural surroundings. On a smaller, more intimate porch (opposite), the French blue door, oyster white siding, and weathered gray decking suggested a darker blue with red, purple, and yellow accents.

With high ceilings, regal columns, and crisp white railings, the classic porch (above) can accommodate floor-to-ceiling curtain panels, which soften the architecture and create the sense of enclosure that turns this space into an outdoor room. White wicker harmonizes with the architecture of the porch and creates crisp frames for blue and green fabrics.

On the small porch (opposite), it's the navy painted canvas rug that gives this pass-through area a roomlike feeling. Accent pillows on the rustic settee pick up colors from the rug, which serves as the focal point for the space.

GREEN

Who can say no to green, the color of nature, hope, and renewal? Newly minted, lime twisted, or sun-drenched, nature's generous green palette heals and refreshes. Did you know that when you look at green, your heart rate slows and you visibly relax? Located at the center of the color spectrum, green represents balance. Rely on it for restful, serene rooms where you can regain your equilibrium.

A one-color-plus-neutrals scheme is a surefire formula for a successfully decorated room because the palette is so straightforward. A midvalue soft green paired with neutrals of about the same lightness or darkness creates a soothing and relaxing mood. This tranquil dining room grows from a base of sisal carpeting. At the center a stone pedestal supports a glass-topped table that reflects the light, helping the small room seem more spacious. A mirrored alcove also visually enlarges the space.

Snowy white trimwork frames the featured green for a crisp, clean look. Lavishing the same color on all the walls and the ceiling unifies the surfaces and visually lowers the ceiling, creating a more intimate mood for dining.

References to the natural world are especially appropriate in a green room. Linen seat slipcovers make vintage dining chairs casually inviting; the color links the chairs to the sisal carpet. The botanical fabric insets on the chairbacks resemble framed art, and an aged-metallic finish dresses up the chair frames, chandelier, and lamps.

Want to rev up the energy in a green scheme? Pick natural-world complements such as floral oranges, reds, and pinks.

COLOR KEY A. walls, ceiling B. trimwork, wainscoting, doors, and built-ins C. chairs D. carpet and chair fabrics

T wo rooms—one with large portions of green, the other with small ones—illustrate two ways to pull off a green color scheme.

What these rooms have in common are dark floors and dark furniture frames as grounding elements. White walls and ceilings assure visual volume and an enhanced sense of space. In spite of these commonalities, the moods of these rooms are quite different. One feels warm and intimate, the other cool, relaxed, and reserved.

To accomplish warm and cozy, as in the dining room (above), expand the green color palette to include neighborly yellow-greens and oranges. Choose a dominant green with a yellow undertone instead of a cool blue one so the other yellow-tone colors easily relate to it. To wrap the colors around the room, draw in darker and lighter versions of the dominant yellow-green, leaving large sections

COLOR KEY A. upholstery, walls, and tablecloth B. ceiling and trimwork C. tablecloth D. draperies and tablecloth E. draperies

of white to maintain spaciousness and to balance the warm hues with a cool factor. Warm, dark wood furniture and honey-tone hardwood flooring offer the perfect foil for the yellow-green palette.

For a cool, serene room (below) choose a light green with blue undertones and use it sparingly, allowing the "uncolors"—white, black, and brown—to take up most of the space. In an envelope absent of color, even small amounts of green have the power to define the room's mood. Dark flooring and black accents offer strength and solidity, securely anchoring the color scheme.

COLOR KEY A. walls, sofa, shutters, and accessories B. chairs and pillows C. wrought-iron furniture frames, picture frame, sculpture D. pillows E. painting and pillows

COLOR KEY A. walls, sofa fabric B. chairs, ceiling, and trimwork C. sofa and seat cushions D. lamps, accessories, pillows, sofa fabric

Although all greens are generally considered calming and healing, each green has a different kind of power. Some, such as mint, pistachio, or jade, refresh and awaken; others, like olive, pine, and avocado, calm and comfort in a quieting way. This room (opposite and above) uses olive green to enclose its inhabitants in security, comfort, and stability.

Olive green paint is made by mixing green and red pigments to obtain a neutralized, earthy hue. In this color scheme, it behaves like dark brown, visually pulling the walls inward and warming the spaces. Red, the natural complement to green, keeps the room from going to sleep. Upholstery pieces covered with red floral prints provide focus and seating that beckons with warmth and comfort. Cool white trimwork, creamy chairs, and pale flooring balance the dark delights of the room, framing deep tones and keeping the space from appearing too dark.

COLOR KEY A. wall, tablecloth, and pillow monogram
B. ceiling, trimwork, and shutters C. upholstery D. painted
floor E. painted floor and accessories F. pillows
G. tablecloth H. painting

This color scheme doesn't follow any of the standard combinations described in this book. It simply skips around the entire color wheel, picking up a saturated hue at every other stop. Starting with an intense but earthy yellow-green, the palette gathers a blue-green, a red-violet, and a red-orange to join the color party. All of the hues have the same saturation and value.

The key to the color mastery? White trimwork, gray flooring, and white furniture pieces provide a neutral backdrop for the four equally intense color companions. Differences in proportion keep the attention-seeking colors from getting out of hand: Lime green gets the feature coverage, allowing accents of blue-green, red-violet, and red-orange to inject lively jolts of energy.

To select saturated colors of the same value (lightness or darkness), squint at the combination. If one "pops" more than the others, choose another value of that color.

t's tempting to begin a color-happy room by choosing the wall color first. However, it's easier (and smarter) to start with fabric or a rug to guide the color choices for the rest of the room.

The upholstered armchair (opposite) provided the inspiration for the wall color in this room. A paint store or home improvement center can mix paint to match your fabric exactly if you take in a swatch to be scanned. A geometric rug that coordinates without matching the chair provides the palette for the remaining furnishings and accessories. Notice how the rug's blues and greens contrast with each other in a playful way. That's a clue for playing blues and greens against each other in the rest of the room—a teal sofa against chartreuse walls, chartreuse throw pillows against teal upholstery, and teal curtains and lampshade against chartreuse walls

To keep the colors in check, black (also a clue from the rug) steps into the room on furniture and curtain rods, balancing the brightness with darkness and anchoring the space with heavy accents. Creamy white on trimwork echoes the rug, providing breathing space around the bright colors and framing them as if they are artwork.

In addition to borrowing color choices from an inspirational piece, maintain its style as well. If the motifs are geometric, as they are in this rug, carry out a geometric theme when you select furniture styles and accessories. If your color inspiration piece is floral or paisley, choose softer, curvier furniture and accessories.

Take color outside. Today's fadeproof, stain-resistant, and worry-free outdoor fabrics make it possible. Every year manufacturers of outdoor fabrics extend and improve their lines of rich colors, innovative patterns, and luscious textures with the soft hand given to indoor fabrics.

You can create an outdoor room in an instant. Like romantic, old-fashioned picnics near a bubbling stream or atop a windy hill (old movies do it best), a laid-back living room can materialize as quickly as a meal in a basket. Check out this chat room under a shady tree. Based on green and blue, the patterned chair cushions jive with the landscape's grassy greens and watery blues. Yellow and orange appear as accents, while a candle chandelier brings overhead lighting out of the house. White wicker crisply frames the upholstery cushions, and white piping delineates the floor cushions.

COLOR KEY A. upholstery and pillows B. furniture and accessories C. upholstery and pillow D. pillows E. pillows

L eafy greens and neutrals tie this porch dining space to the surrounding landscape. Almost more yellow than green, the main color—pistachio—is supported by the moss green hue painted on the floor. Like grass, the moss green color has a neutralizing effect that grounds the space while showcasing the light, bright enamel of the furniture.

It's a simple scheme, a no-brainer inspired by the greens and yellow-greens of nature. To pump it up, the head chair is painted a bright yellow.

To paint a porch floor, use porch and deck paint on clean, smoothly sanded, and dustless floorboards. Colors at your home improvement center may be limited, but you can custom-order the color you want, using white porch paint as the base. To protect the painted floor, cover it with several coats of clear polyurethane. Another option: durable, waterproof marine paint.

Lest the green scheme melt away into the green background, kiss it with temporary complements pulled out for a garden party—red-hot fuchsias, oranges, and reds. They make great fruit, flower, and tablesetting color choices.

COLOR KEY A. chairs, table, and tablecoverings
B. painted floor C. tablecloth and porch trimwork
D. head chair

Browns make color schemes work. Like lovely bridges between pure colors, they end color conflicts and bring peace to every room. But make no mistake—brown isn't just brown. With a glorious palette of its own, brown appears as nature's neutrals—mink, clay, oak, stone, oatmeal, linen, and cinnamon. Use these comfortable hues to ground every room of your home.

BROW

Drink in this frothy mix of creamy latte, cappuccino, and espresso hues. Like a hot cup of coffee, these classic browns are sure to comfort a bedroom and its inhabitants any time of the day.

With the right proportions of light, medium, and dark tones, a monochromatic palette can create a stylish country, modern, or traditional atmosphere. In this modern bedroom, brown walls and carpet are balanced by a white ceiling and a wall of white sheers, avoiding the cavelike feeling that a room filled with brown walls could create. The textured bedding connects the bed to the window wall. Countering the lightness of the window and bedding are a midtone café au lait carpet, Eurostyle square pillows, and grass-cloth walls, which warm and balance the pale surfaces. Dark espresso used in small amounts on the duvet and accent pillows delivers a dramatic punch to the scheme.

Don't forget metals in a one-color scheme. Silver or platinum is a good color for a cool, modern style. A traditional bedroom often looks best with gold-color metals.

COLOR KEY A. wall and carpet B. bedding, draperies, ceiling, lampshades, and accessories C. bedding and carpet D. pillows E. pillow

COLOR KEY A. walls B. chair covers C. ceiling and chandelier D. mirror frame and crown and base moldings

Like the bedroom on pages 124–125, this dining room also carries a tonal palette. The results are different because the main brown is golden, and the proportions of light, medium, and dark browns favor light and medium tones. While the bedroom seems cool and open, the dining room is warm and deep.

Another big difference: Inspired by the rich spaces of old-world English manors, every surface in this luxurious dining room is treated with heavy texture. Stucco walls, woodgrain furniture, monogrammed linen slipcovers, carved frames, faceted glass, and a woven carpet fascinate the eye and appeal to the sense of touch.

Why aren't the crown moldings and baseboards the same color as the window frames? The paint color, drawn from the multitone sponged walls, makes the walls seem taller. Dark frames would have visually shortened the room, creating a crowded feeling.

COLOR KEY A. walls, bedding, canopy, table skirt, draperies B. trimwork, quilt, and benches C. duvet cover, bench cushions, flowerpot D. ceiling accent stripe, bedding, and headboard E. carpet, ceiling, bedding, and lampshades

Colors quickly shift moods under different types of light—natural, halogen, fluorescent, or incandescent. Pale blue, the queen of tranquillity, can look pretty on a paint chip but feel chilly on walls and furnishings under cool-white or low lights. What's the antidote if you want a restful blue in your bedroom? Mix in the magic touch of brown.

This bedroom features big doses of golden brown coupled with a cool, watery blue hue. The colors balance under almost all types of illumination, especially in a room with lots of natural light. The trick is to choose browns and blues with the same value so light and dark contrasts don't play into the scheme. Then be sure to include soft and easy patterns, such as these stripes and checks, to provide plenty of variations and fields of interest for the eye.

COLOR KEY A. walls, carpet, sofa, ottomans B. accent wall, draperies, shades, chairs, carpet, lampshade, and pillows C. draperies and pillows D. ceiling and paper lampshade

Don't deny yourself chocolate, the trendy craving that inspires so many color schemes. Paired with a sweet confectionary blue hue, chocolate brown is stirring up tasteful rooms.

Love the chocolate idea but don't dare to dip in too much? Start with an accent wall. Balance it with light beige walls, sisal carpets, linen upholstery, and wood or bamboo blinds. Take the space from neutral to lively wth shots of pastel blue on fabrics and tabletops. In this room, circles inspired by the upholstery fabric of the chairs have been applied to the chocolate wall, turning it into a work of art. The round shapes counter the straight lines of the room and create a feeling of movement. Round plates with circular motifs continue the flow on a secondary wall.

Earthtones never go out of fashion. The soft hues step easily from century to century and from home to home, making them excellent choices for long-term color scheming. In these living rooms, in-tune tones create the same calm, harmonic mood, despite their color and style differences.

The traditional take on living (above) combines muted mocha upholstery and soft cinnamon draperies with walls coated in a honeyed tan and outlined with fresh white woodwork. A light oatmeal color rug lifts and lightens the space, while wood pieces with red undertones anchor it. In this warm, mostly neutral space, the deep blue of the artwork makes a dramatic focal point.

COLOR KEY A. walls and sofa B. carpet C. chair upholstery D. draperies E. ceiling and trimwork F. artwork

In the contemporary living room (below) the large uncluttered space focuses attention on the island of earthtone furnishings. A patterned rug carrying all of the colors of the palette grounds a velvety chocolate-color sofa. Clean-lined wooden tables echo the straight lines of the sofa and the home's architecture for a minimalist look. The quiet neutrals and natural colors encourage the eye to take in the green garden view framed by pale green linen draperies. The beige chair is almost invisible in the space.

COLOR KEY A. wall, chair, and rug B. sofa, rug, coffee table C. pillows and rug D. draperies

S it down with brown and let its comforting arms embrace you. Organic as the earth itself, brown travels back to nature, taking you with it. Family rooms, sitting rooms, reading rooms, and dens are perfect places to try your hand at restful brown-driven color schemes.

Inspired by the colors of the reading chair upholstery fabric, the palette for this sitting room is simple: dark and light browns, white, and cream, with turquoise as a focal point and accent color. From the ground up, cream and white frame the brown walls and furniture colors. The pale colors also provide enough light to keep the space livable. Mostly modern furniture and accessory shapes cue in to a retro-1950s style, but the warmth of the colors and textures takes the edge off what could be a slick, stark modernity.

When painting walls dark brown, prime them first with a dark primer. Otherwise you'll have to apply multiple coats to get good color coverage.

COLOR KEY A. walls, pillows, ottoman, chair, lamps, and accessories B. sofa, chair, art, and accessories C. carpet D. trimwork, blinds, and chair E. chair and pillow

COLOR KEY A. walls and wicker furniture B. stone flooring C. seat cushions D. coffee table and pillow E. pillows and accessories F. pillows and throw

D ecorating is like putting together a fashionable look from your closet. First you mix or match the basics. Then you add eyecatching accessories to bring the look to life.

This outdoor scheme takes its cue from the exterior of the house. In a seamless transition, the furniture appears in the same colors as the stucco walls. Beige upholstery, wicker seating, ottomans, and brick flooring continue the midtone hue and offer the building blocks of comfortable seating. Open to the air on two sides, the room benefits from large doses of sunshine that bring the brown surfaces to light.

Like memorable wardrobe accessories, shots of pink, orange, yellow, and green pop against the beiges. Pillows, plastic outdoor rugs, and accent furniture pieces—the coffee table and buffet—are the jewelry of this room. A pair of candelabras above the fireplace make this space feel as comfortable as any indoor living area.

GRAY

The chic sophisticate of color scheming, gray is the genie that appears as a whiff of smoke one minute and solid rock the next. Born of nature, it's hard as granite, concrete, and stone; shiny as silver, aluminum, and lead; soft as a silver fox; grainy as driftwood. Explore the subtleties of charcoal grays and gray greens. Use grays to neutralize, sanitize, and solidify your color schemes.

L ike a gray flannel suit with Edwardian lines, this bedroom
stands apart from the usual crowd of sleeping spaces. Crisp
and clean, tailored and textured, the room is a quiet zone,
cool and still as the night.

Compare this bedroom to the brown bedroom on pages 124–125
for differences in temperature and mood. The brown bedroom,
connected to the natural world beyond its draperies, exudes warmth
and casual elegance. This room turns inward, insulating itself from the
outside world in a cool and formal way.

In a nearly one-color gray scheme such as this, adding texture
invites your mind and eye to enjoy subtle surfaces. These walls are
lined with silk, and the headboard draperies are a lovely light wool.
The white carpet contrasts with the polished mahogany bed; the
bedding is as crisp and clean as a starched white shirt. And who
wouldn't want to sit in the luxury of the platinum satin chair? Using
a one-color scheme is a great way to build decorating confidence.
Instead of worrying about mixing multiple hues, you're free to
concentrate on layering tints and shades of the same color and
adding textures to make them shine.

COLOR KEY A. walls B. draperies and headboard
drapery C. bedding, ceiling, trimwork, carpet, lampshade
D. chair

COLOR KEY A. sofa, chairs, ottoman, and coffee table B. walls, carpet, and upholstery C. ceiling, trimwork, chair, lampshades D. pillows and accessories

s a chic gray color scheme destined to be cold and reserved? Definitely not. Gray can be warm or cool, depending on how it's made. Grays that have blue undertones yield coolness, but those based on yellow or red are as warm as pebbles on a sunny beach. You can use warm grays to balance cool ones.

If you love the ease of working with neutrals, mix cool grays with browns for a sophisticated yet friendly living room. Quiet and elegant, this space comes together in a neutral palette and a pleasing mix of furnishings. Plush slipper chairs covered in gray linen keep company with a walnut coffee table and vintage Chinese desk. Pale gray carpet and accent pieces underscore the cushy depths of the seating pieces, contrasting with their darkness and keeping the weight of the furniture from visually sinking into the floor. Black-and-white photographs and a mirror also counter with cool, contemporary flair and shine.

The Swedes know how to flood a room with subtle colors, a light sense of history, and quiet elegance. The secret to their success: something new, something old, and a pale color scheme based on neutrals and a single accent color.

Antique gray furnishings provide the historical context and architecture for this dining room. While the receding dove gray is secondary to buttermilk white, it's the darkest hue in the space (except for the wood floor) and therefore subtly anchors the color scheme. Gray chair frames outline white linen upholstery. Two shades of gray color the antique mirror over the buffet, and the curvaceous gray clock stands like a sentinel at the side of the room. The pale yellow wall and tablecloth color choices were inspired by the yellow tones of the antique sideboard.

COLOR KEY A. walls, tablecloth, detailing on buffet B. mirror frame C. clock, chair frames, mirror frame D. ceiling, trimwork, shutters, tablecloth, seat cushions, accessories E. detailing on buffet

Sometimes gray is so warm-toned that it looks brown, especially when paired with rust. Check out the gray paint chips at a home improvement center to learn about this versatile neutral. You'll find a great range—from warm yellow-grays to cool purple-grays—that skirts the entire color wheel. Mixed by crossing complements or adding black or white to basic hues, the possibilities for gray are endless. So are the benefits.

The biggest benefit of gray? Its ability to compromise. Gray's appeal is also timeless, lending itself to any single decorating style or marriage of two. This room blends two opposing decorating passions—one contemporary, with a preference for edgy furniture and lots of black, the other fond of floral patterns and antiques. Warm-tone grays bridge the differences and bind the distinct styles together.

COLOR KEY A. walls, toile wallcovering, shades B. sofa, hutch, and accessories C. ceiling, trimwork, shutters, and pillows D. lampshades, coffee table, and accessories E. pillows

COLOR KEY A. walls B. chimney, fireplace stone, and accessories C. trimwork, carpet, and lampshades D. sectional sofa E. pillows F. pillows

Gray and cream schemes produce wonderful results, no matter what the style. In the contemporary living room (opposite), a soaring 20-foot-high vaulted ceiling produces volume that could seem empty and unfriendly, but the beamed maple ceiling makes the space feel more intimate. While crisp white paint sets off the gray grid above the fireplace surround, driftwood gray stain on maple cabinetry and paint on the walls balance with warmth. More warmth comes from orange and red cushions on the green sectional.

The cozy ambience of the traditional room (above right) comes from sand-color walls, gold accents, luxurious textures, and a purple-gray hue that visually lowers the ceiling to cozy the room. A dark chair, picture frame, and fireplace surround offer contrasts to the light hues, giving the room a balanced feel.

COLOR KEY A. walls B. ceiling C. chair D. chaise longue, carpet, throw, and trimwork E. pillow

COLOR KEY (above) **A.** chairs, table, curtains, shelf, and accessories **B.** wall **C.** vases and artwork **D.** chairs and vases

Living in an outdoor space comes easy with gray—think of the possibilities! Concrete pavers, stone walkways, gravel groundcovers, deck materials that resemble weathered driftwood, and clay pots for plants are just a few of the naturally gray materials you can parlay into an outdoor living room. Add a few manufactured grays—resin or metal chairs, stone or concrete water fountains, marble tables, area rugs, cushions, and solution-dyed acrylic curtains that withstand the effects of the sun and rain—and you have all the comforts of an indoor room. With your gray structure grounded and a mix of textural furnishings in place, decorate your outdoor room with fresh greens—grass green, bamboo, and limey tones—plus a punch of white here and there. If you want to rev up the color scheme, simply add bright flowers from your local garden center or your own garden.

The two outdoor rooms on these pages use similar color palettes but exhibit different lifestyles. The dining room (opposite) includes a carefully orchestrated group of contemporary furnishings in a well-protected outdoor space. Like an indoor dining room, it has all the luxuries of refinement—art, artful table settings, and filmy curtains. The dining room (below) is styled with casual pieces and greenhouse-glass walls, suggesting that living and dining outdoors is a spontaneous affair that connects immediately and intimately with the natural world around it. Which do you like best?

COLOR KEY (below) A. table and deck B. chairs and vase C. upholstery, tableware, and table runner D. upholstery and pillows

COLOR KEY A. chair upholstery B. wrought-iron furniture C. pillows D. pillows

Color schemes for patios and outdoor spaces start with the colors of the house exterior. The cool gray and white of the pergola and the gray-brown mahogany deck create a quiet, sophisticated backdrop for outdoor furnishings.

Black wrought-iron furniture and taupe weather-worthy cushions blend with the architectural colors to preserve the understated effect. Pale celadon accent pillows add the barest whisper of color to the setting. On such a neutral stage, you can add a temporary pick-me-up with any brilliant fruit or flower color—fuchsia, orange, red, lime green, purple, blue, or yellow.

B&W

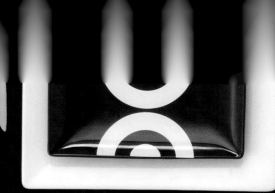
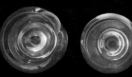

Different as night and day, black and white support the theory that opposites attract. Together they're inseparable, lending sophistication and glamour to any decorating scheme. Not quite ready to cover your walls with contrasting stripes? Start small. Add a black shade to a white lamp, or cover a floor with a black-and-white rug. As your color confidence grows, incorporate new contrasts to the room.

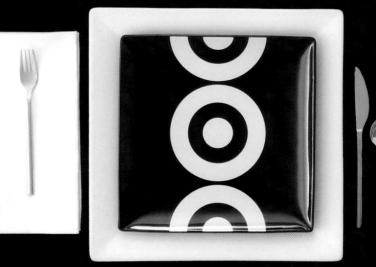

This living room represents a way to get comfortable with black-and-white color scheming—use the decorating duo on focal point pieces, then surround them with softer whites and warm-feeling neutrals to make the black-and-white items (and you) feel at home. Here the color combo makes artworks stand out when it's accompanied by creamy-beige upholstery fabrics, gold-tone draperies, pale walls, and rusty-red accent pillows.

Black's role in this scheme is to draw thin, artful lines, while white creates a backdrop for the black elements. These proportions—a little black and lots of white—always work. Black's strength easily overpowers a room while white's receding nature is comfortable in large doses. This makes white the perfect background color for black. Use white to set the stage for a show-off black that quickly brings drama to a room.

COLOR KEY A. wall, sofa, and accessories B. accessories
C. upholstery and draperies D. carpet and accessories E. pillows

156

n the world of black and white, submissive white is the easier hue to manage and live with. To gain color confidence, start with white—an entire room of it!

This room's simple charms and surprising drama make it fascinating. Charm comes from rustic furnishings already in the room, and the color drama is born of a great wash of white. White contrasts with the natural woodtones to delineate them and visually opens the space to create an airy atmosphere. The result? A monastic yet fresh, clean space that reflects confidence and taste. It answers color questions with one phrase: White is always right.

White's role in any room is to transform, cleanse, lift, and visually expand it. White walls give you a fresh canvas for new decorating decisions; use them to revamp rooms cluttered with a previous owner's colors after you move into a home. Use white on upholstery or washable slipcovers; they'll connect seamlessly with white walls to create unity in the room. When collecting, limit your color choices to one—white. A row of ironstone plates on the mantel (left) transforms a simple collection into a design statement.

COLOR KEY A. walls, upholstery, fireplace, trimwork, and accessories B. rug and baskets C. fire screen

COLOR KEY (right) A. walls, desk, and accessories
B. floor and accessories C. window shades and chair slip
D. chair

COLOR KEY (opposite) A. ceiling, upholstery, trimwork,
mantel, pillow B. walls, lampshade, pillow C. chairs, rug,
coffee table, side table, and accessories D. carpet, window
shade, and accessories E. pillow and accessories

Simple but not spartan; sophisticated but not snooty—black-and-white color schemes can feel downright cozy. These rooms look clean but not cold thanks to a few decorating tricks. Here's how you can do it:

Control the color. An ebony-and-white palette creates instant drama and simplicity. Trim rooms with warm neutrals and steer clear of too many accent colors. Khaki walls and sea-grass flooring warm the room (opposite); a leather chair slip and bamboo shades do the same for the office area (above).

Choose organic materials to add familiar comforts. Use wood that's unfinished, painted, wire-brushed, or stained to subtly reveal its grain and texture. Avoid brushed stainless steel, polished chrome, highly polished ceramic tile, and glass surfaces that cool the temperature in the room. Accent with natural items such as plants, seashells, flowers, and fruit.

Ready to try your hand at black-and-white upholstery or wallcoverings? Just a few bold patterns are needed to command a room when it's filled with contrasting colors, elegant textures, and clean-lined furnishings. Dominating the room with its scrollwork pattern, the bench at the head of this table is supported by two rows of guest chairs. At the other end, a black bench balances the weight of the scrollwork print.

The rest of the room is enveloped in a simple scheme of brown and white—dark at floor level, light above. Countering the spare, contemporary presentation of furnishings, white-painted wainscoting on cream-painted walls offers a hint of traditional style. Sparkle comes from an antique chandelier and reflective surfaces. The main colors—white, black, and brown—invite bright bouquets of flowers that are temporary and easily changed from one occasion to the next.

COLOR KEY A. walls B. upholstery, table C. upholstery, wainscoting, sheers, and accessories D. draperies, pillow

Black-and-white color schemes allow you to use strong accent colors. Use yellow to make black and white appear happy, orange to get them singing, or red to bring out passion. If you blend black and white with blue, green, or purple, the room temperature moves to the cooler end of the spectrum and the mood will be serious, sophisticated, or reflective.

In this sunny room, strokes of black and white frame and ground the brash, bold yellow and lime green focal point colors. The happy scheme balances light and dark, masculine and feminine. A jazzy mix of vibrant lines—from a folksy rug to a framed flea-market scarf (cleverly resembling a modern ink print)—emits even more positive energy. The woven lines of the white waffle-pattern fruit bowl and black midcentury modern chair create large textures, bringing more interest and lively feeling to the room.

COLOR KEY A. walls, rug, tables, and accessories B. rug, artwork, pillow, and accessories C. sofa D. window shade and throw

The outdoor color ideas here show you how to move beyond the confines of a porch or outdoor room limited by walls. Outdoor living steps down and out to the garden, where walls of green create the setting for the neutral decorating palette.

Barely-there color—white, putty, slate, black, and brown—brings a feeling of relaxation and rest to the space. The slate patio, two steps down from the wood deck attached to the house, is both beautiful and practical. The raw nature of the stone grounds a secondary seating area. When decorating out in the open like this, buy outdoor wicker furniture and cushions with fabrics made to weather summer storms; store the outdoor furnishings in snowy months.

COLOR KEY A. siding, tables, pillows, and accessories B. furniture C. decking D. cushions E. blinds, lampshades, and accessories

COLOR FOR THE WHOLE HOUSE

THE HEART RESPONDS TO HARMONY

In your romance with color and your search for just the right hues, you want the color choices throughout your home to connect to each other. If you can see one room from another, the relationships of the colors between the rooms will affect your comfort level. Unrelated colors jar the senses, while related colors answer the heart's desire for harmony and a peaceful flow from room to room. The houses in this chapter untangle color conflicts and answer questions about how to connect your rooms with color, what colors to paint your trim, and how to develop a whole-house color scheme.

OPEN PLAN:
TWO COLORS + BLACK & TAN

When the front door opens on the rooms of an open plan home, the color palette for the whole house is apparent at first glance. The color scheme must be singularly strong, moving easily from room to room without a hitch.

To be sure of harmony, rely heavily on neutrals to cover most of the territory. This high-contrast palette joins black and tan. Tan becomes the main wall color and one of the ceiling colors (see page 173). Black, the powerful one, creates drama and excitement on furnishings. Partnering silently (and equally) with black, white does the work of defining the architecture and covering most ceilings.

You could stop there—neutral colors make a fine scheme. But for color lovers, hues that bring verve and vitality are a must. Use them as accents and mood-makers without going overboard—too much of a good thing could spoil the effect. A complementary pairing of lime green and red-orange gets the supporting color role at this house. Inspired by the pear painting in the great-room, green is the accent

COLOR KEY (PAGES 170–173) A. walls, ceiling, backsplash, and upholstery B. trimwork, ceiling, and cabinetry C. wood furniture, rug, and accessories D. walls, upholstery, pillows, and accessories E. chairs and accessories F. upholstery and artwork

color in fabrics and accessories. Red-orange joins the party in smaller doses on fabrics and artwork.

Green takes the lead in the entry/breakfast area, enlivening this narrow passage and introducing the whole-house color scheme. Views into the great-room offer glimpses of lime green that draw the eye into that space. Red-orange debuts in the hallway in the artwork that lines the walls, while black and tan, so prominent in the great-room, play a minor role, appearing on the rug and breakfast set.

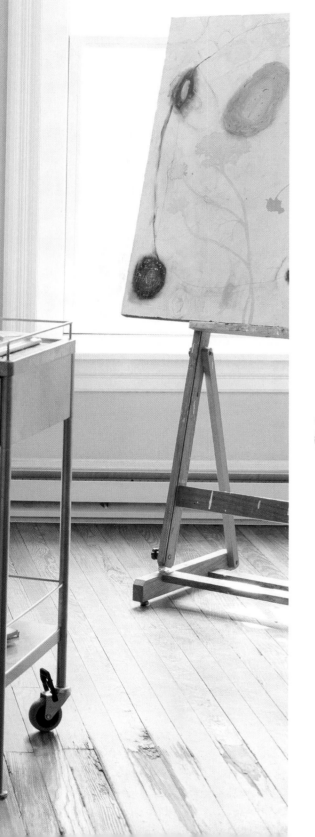

ARTIST IN RESIDENCE:
A SYMPHONY OF COLOR

What is the secret to transforming an old house with traditional features into a chic, sophisticated, and modern family home? Liberal use of light colors—with different retro-pastel wall tones in every room—combined with bright-white trim. When it comes to furnishings, work within a limited range of colors—mustard yellows, pinks, greens, browns, and blacks. If you buy individual pieces you love in these hues, everything will work together throughout the house.

The strategy for the look—midcentury modern meets American farmhouse—is to do no harm to the original dwelling. In this home painted walls and new lighting fixtures are the only alterations to the structure. The same bright-white paint brushes the trimwork, ceilings, and walls above the picture moldings, linking the rooms together and creating pristine frames for the pastel tones of the rooms. Once new fixtures shed light on the freshened walls, the color-limited furnishings fall into place.

COLOR KEY (PAGES 174–177) A. upholstery, chair, and accessories B. trimwork, ceilings, bedding, and accessories C. walls, accessories D. walls, accessories E. walls and bedding F. rug, chair, and accessories G. chairs

Much of the color scheming comes to a finish with furnishings and accessories. For example, the mustard yellow of a vintage neobaroque sofa in the living room (pages 174–175) makes a color statement against pale gray walls. In the adjacent dining room (above) a pink, black, and brown scheme originates with paintings and chairs. In the master bedroom (opposite) a pistachio quilt and pillows repeat the green of the walls. Altogether the separate color notes of the house combine in a symphonic whole.

EARTHTONES:
MAKING COLORFUL TRANSITIONS

Sometimes a home has two or three trimwork and flooring colors—white, birch, and cherry or oak. Although several woods are consistent throughout the house, they act more as accents and accessories than unifying elements. If this is the case in your home, use a transitional wall color to link your rooms.

An earthy green appears as the unifying element of this traditional-modern home. Comfortable as green fields on a horizon, it appears in every space and through every doorway. You'll find it on hallway walls, on upper-level surfaces seen from the first floor, and as a bathroom color viewed from the master bed. The calming color flows easily from space to space without blowing its horn, allowing other colors to vie for attention as accents and mood creators.

The green transition invites other earthy hues to the palette— they're needed for contrast, excitement, and playfulness. In the gathering space shown here, a brownish red complements the field

COLOR KEY (PAGES 178–181) A. walls B. walls and pillows C. walls D. walls and bedding E. trimwork and accessories F. upholstery

green transitions, adding warmth to spaces where appetites and conversations come together. Straw yellow appears as an accent in the same social spaces and in the powder room (opposite).

When it comes to sleeping, the desired mood is one of rest and relaxation, so a smoky blue is brushed onto the walls of the master bedroom (above). The transitional green reappears in the sunny master bathroom.

GARDEN FRESH:
A MULTICOLOR PALETTE

R osy pinks, butter yellows, apple greens, and periwinkle blues—plucked from an English cottage garden—create a pastel palette for a sweet-and-easy home. White trim throughout the house smooths the transition from room to room and frames the garden colors.

Color is key to the home's easy visual flow. The same seven colors appear in all of the rooms. However, they appear in different proportions in each space, allowing for mood changes. For example, the butter yellow walls of the living room combine with soft pink upholstery and floral draperies for a classic cottage look. The yellow walls continue into the dining room (visible through the kitchen doorway on page 184) where a glittering crystal chandelier suggests a romantic and more formal mood. By comparison, the casual kitchen (page 184), with crisp periwinkle walls and lime green cabinets, feels

COLOR KEY (PAGES 182–185) A. walls, accessories
B. walls, accessories C. walls, dresser, accessories
D. trimwork, ceiling, bedding, countertops, and accessories
E. cabinetry and accessories F. draperies, shades, bedding,
pillows, upholstery, accessories G. rugs and accessories

brisk and cheerful. Thanks to cool green, the bedroom (opposite) has a restful mood. The lesson for you? By changing the dominant hue in each room, you can create a different mood or personality to fit the function of the space.

Fabrics that carry this garden color palette assist in changing the moods of the rooms: Floor-length chintz draperies and toile introduce formal overtones to the living and dining area, while curtains in the kitchen and adjoining breakfast area are decidedly informal. Luxurious layers in the bedroom add up to a cozy feel.

COLOR TO THE RESCUE:
CRAYON BOX TRANSFORMATION

This house shows how a piece of art can inspire a whole-house scheme. The painting above the living room fireplace, glimpsed through the kitchen's peekaboo cutout windows, provides the cue for many of the colors used to transform a once-dull ranch-style house into a vibrant showplace. A sliver of yellow in the painting suggested the yellow ocher that covers the living and dining room walls. Light gray-blue shapes inspired the hue on the kitchen wall. The deeper blues and light and dark greens in the absract piece are echoed in tiles and on upholstery fabrics. Red isn't in the painting, but as the complement of green it serves as the primary accent color in every room.

The engaging palette—a sophisticated variation on crayon hues—and a judicious balance of vivid and restrained brights give the 1950s house a strong design presence and a heaping dose of color.

To avoid chaos, one color dominates each space. In the kitchen,

COLOR KEY (PAGES 186–189) A. walls, backsplash, accessories B. walls, backsplash C. trimwork, ceiling, countertops, pendent lights, accessories D. upholstery, backsplash, and accessories E. upholstery and accessories F. upholstery and accessories

it's the gray-blue; in the living and dining area, it's the yellow ocher. In the kitchen, mosaic tiles in dark, medium, and light blue and yellow ocher make the connection to the painting—and they're repeated on the hearth in the living room to cement the link.

In the living and dining area, green, blue, and red upholstery and accessories balance each other in fairly equal amounts. White accents mediate between the strong colors and add crispness to the scheme.

COLOR TALK:
ANSWERS TO QUESTIONS ABOUT WORKING WITH COLOR

The houses on the previous pages illustrate five distinct ways you can handle whole-house color scheming: a limited high-contrast palette for an open plan; a pastel palette that creates a color statement in each room; an earthtone palette hinged on a transitional hue; a multicolor palette that sets up a dialogue between rooms; and a crayon box palette managed by light and a balance of vivid and restrained brights.

To learn more about choosing and using color, read on for the answers to frequently asked questions.

1 WHAT IF I WANT TO USE A LOT OF COLORS? Choose your colors in the same value so they relate easily to each other. This avoids high contrasts, which are more difficult to balance. Use one of the colors as a dominant feature in each room and accessorize with the remaining colors.

2 HOW CAN I CREATE WHOLE-HOUSE CONTINUITY? Three methods: 1) Paint or stain all of the trim the same color throughout your house. 2) Use a thread of the same hue in every room; the repetition will link them. 3) Use a limited palette with two or three related colors in varying amounts from room to room.

3 DOES LIGHT AFFECT COLOR? Yes. Every color looks pure in natural light. In ample sunlight vivid colors may seem less brilliant. Under artificial light they may appear heavy. Because you can't predict which colors are best for your situation, do color tests before investing in paint or expensive upholstery fabrics. Paint large swatches on walls and borrow fabric swatches from stores to view the colors in the rooms where you will be using them. See how the colors look at various times of the day and under different lighting conditions before committing to paint and fabric.

4 HOW CAN COLOR CONNECT MY ROOMS? Color is the "glue" in any cohesive decorating plan, fastening the rooms together. You'll need one or more colors to bridge the gap between adjoining rooms. The scheme can shift as long as any two adjoining rooms have a color in common.

5 WHAT COLORS ENHANCE WOOD FURNITURE? Consider the dominant hues in the wood finish and whether you prefer the drama of high contrast or the subtle richness of low-contrast schemes. Against pale walls, dark and red-grained woods stand out. Against dark walls, dark woods blend in and light ones stand out.

6 HOW DO I WORK WITH THE COLOR OF MY BRICK? To integrate a brick feature into a scheme, decide whether you want to focus attention on it or blend it in. If you like the color of the brick, treat it like any paint or fabric color and use the color wheel to find harmonious companion hues. If you don't like the color, you may wish to paint the brick. Match it to the room's woodwork to emphasize its role as an architectural feature. Or paint it the same color as the walls to make it disappear into the background.

7 SHOULD MOLDINGS BE A DIFFERENT COLOR? If your moldings are wide, unusual, or surround architectural features you'd like to emphasize, paint them a hue that contrasts with the walls. If they are nondescript, make them disappear by painting them the same color as the walls.

8 HOW CAN I KEEP MY COLORS UP-TO-DATE? Invest in timeless, rather than trendy, big-ticket furnishings, emphasizing neutrals or fairly muted colors. Then choose less-expensive items—paint, fabrics, and accessories—in the colors you currently love. When the desire to change a color scheme comes, make changes to the paint, fabrics, and accessories.

9 WHAT COLOR SHOULD I PAINT MY CEILINGS? Ceilings painted a lighter color than the walls feel higher; darker ceilings feel lower. White or a light color is a good choice for an airy, spacious feel. A contrasting color alters the architecture dramatically. To wrap your room in cozy color, paint the ceiling the same color as the walls.

INDEX

perk up
your home

ADT0290_1107